Life Will Find You Again

Annette Herd

Life Will Find You Again

Life Will Find You Again
ISBN 978 1 76041 009 4
Copyright © Annette Herd 2015

First published 2015 by
GINNINDERRA PRESS
PO Box 3461 Port Adelaide SA 5015
www.ginninderrapress.com.au

Contents

A Dream	7
A Man of Wondrous Talent	8
Ageless I am	9
An Eyelash	10
Arkaroola	11
Bonded	12
Bush-flies	13
Bushfire	14
Can't	15
Dementia	16
Desert	17
Easy to Die	18
Fragile	19
Freedom	20
Her Mother	21
His Holiness	22
How Much	23
Let Me Heal	25
Life Will Find You Again	26
Love Endures	28
Morning Walks	29
Most Days	30
Mother Talk	31
My Silence	32
No Such Thing	33
Oh World, Retreat	34
Puppy's First Walk	36
Regrets	38
Siberia	39
So Be It	40

Strong	42
The Bonds of Guilt	43
The Bridges of Madison County	44
The Gift of Menopause	45
The Gift of Silence	46
Their Land We Walk	47
Threesome	49
Too Old, Too Short	50
Turned to Stone	51
Widow	52
Winter Sun	53

A Dream

I had a dream.

Once.

What dream?

I must have dreamt it.

A Man of Wondrous Talent

I look at him in the reverse
As we converse in front of the big wall of mirrors.
He listens attentively to my ideas and concerns,
Offers options and suggestions.
He guides me from short to long and back again
With variations of medium in between.
He navigates the ups and downs, corners and straights
Of my follicle landscape with skill and dedication.
He is a man of wondrous talent.
Thanks to him I like what meets me in my mirror.

Ageless I am

When I look into the mirror
I see
An ageing body
Wrinkles and waistline
Greying hair and glasses

When I create
I am
A fearless vessel of ideas
An instrument of possibilities
An ageless atom dancing with the universe.

An Eyelash

After you had gone
I found an eyelash of yours.
Long and curved.
Dark against the white of the basin.
I saw you standing there
Combing your hair
Washing your face
Looking at yourself in the mirror.

I sat on the edge of the seat
And gave way to mourning.

Arkaroola

Sun pierces winter air.
Everywhere I look
Explosions of native colour.
For the fraction
Of an optical degree
The world of man
Ceases to exist.
In its place creation,
Pristine and pure.
The permanent peace
Of countless rising suns
On red rock.

Bonded

I hurt you.
You hurt me.

I blame you.
You blame me.

I disappoint you.
You disappoint me.

I judge you.
You judge me.

I fail you.
You fail me.

I try.
You try.

Parted by differences.

Bonded by blood.

We battle on.

Bush-flies

The flies are very friendly here.
They share your tea, they share your beer,
And with much jollity and cheer
They settle in your eye and ear.

They buzz around you all day long
Singing their low-pitched buzzing song
Immune to ointment, spray or pong.
Science's got this one very wrong.

So in the end you ditch your pride
And don a net to save your hide,
But even if it's tightly tied,
There's always one that gets inside.

Bushfire

Sky glows orange over an anxious night.
Sun rises over blackened bush.
Day dawns on devastation.
Exhaustion blankets men and women.
Loss will be looked at later.
The battle is not won yet.

Can't

Can't live my life because I love you.
I have to do what's right for me.
Can't make a choice because I'm with you.
I'll pay the price, I'll face the fee.

I cannot ask you for permission
To do the things I need to do.
You say you gave me lots of freedom.
I don't think that is up to you.

Can't sit around and wait forever
For you to join me on my ride.
The river runs or it goes stagnant.
You either face life or you hide.

I cannot hope that you will change.
I have not got the right to ask.
But I can't hang around and stay.
I want a life without a mask.

Dementia

We went to see Opa in the nursing home.
A wreck in a chair.
A shell of a man.

A foot moving restlessly
without control or conscious thought,
in beat with my son's
hard and silent sobs,
and my aching guilt.

God knows where my father has gone.
I wish his body followed.

Desert

Naked under the serenity of distant stars
Enveloped by the vastness of red dirt
I listen to the heartbeat of the Universe
Like a child in the womb of Space
And embrace the solitude of Mother Earth
Life will take me back to
Cities and mobile phones
Taxes, water rates and payment plans
But in this tiny pocket of eternity called Now
I melt into the grains of sand between my feet
And for one tiny fraction of a moment
I am one.

Easy to Die

It occurs to me

That it would be easy to die.

As easy as to fade into darkness like the sinking sun on my back.
As easy as to be eroded by the wind like the dune I am sitting on.

As easy as to be washed away by the waves like my footprints on the sand.

I would simply regress into the watery womb of the sea and dissolve.

My body would feed the fish and my life would finally have purpose.

Fragile

We are fragile, you and I
No matter how hard we try
There is always something to divide us.
I find faults in you
You find faults in me
On occasion we forget what binds us.

We soldier on regardless.
Like astronauts in outer space
Where gravity means nothing
And there's nothing to hold onto
Except the hope that our ropes won't break.
We soldier on.

I lie awake at night
I watch you in the light
That floats in through the bedroom window.
I see your chest rise and fall
I ask myself, if this is all
Life has to offer day by day.

We soldier on regardless.
Like astronauts in outer space
Where gravity means nothing
And there's nothing to hold onto
Except the hope that our ropes won't break.
We soldier on.

Freedom

I am free to learn
Free to take the wrong turn
Be obnoxious or bold
Warm-hearted or cold
Behave like a fool
Be totally uncool
Be stubborn and wrong
Free to burst into song
Even if I don't get it right
Free to quarrel and fight
Free to make a wrong choice
Free not to care if I voice
An opinion that's fraught
We all live to be taught
And to learn from mistakes
Which everyone makes
And who gives a dime
That every line
Ends on a rhyme
In this poem of mine!

Her Mother

She did not hold
But needed to be held
Daggers of reproach
Dramas of ill proportion
Demanding like a two-year-old
A child to her children
Living out her days
Surrounded by obligation

His Holiness

He held my hands in his.
Soft, warm, gentle hands.
Head bent in a humble bow
He acknowledged my thanks.
If ever there was a human being
Capable of unconditional love
It was him in this very moment
When he held my hands.
His touch can't have lasted more
Than half a minute.
His loving kindness will be with me
For a lifetime.

How Much

How much

Can I

Turn
To make you happy

Go against my grain
To toe your line

Pretend I agree
To keep you smiling

Show I care
To meet your needs

Offer you love
To fill your well

Bend over backwards
To pick you up

Bow before you
To satisfy your expectations

Give you my attention
To appease your grudges

Force myself to listen
To smooth out your resentment

Open my mouth
To fuel your conversation

How much

Must I

Disintegrate

To make you whole.

Let Me Heal

Let me stay here a while
Turn the clock face to the wall
Let me rest and catch my breath
Bathe me in the scent of grass
Let autumn warmth lull me to sleep
Whilst I retrieve lost segments of my soul
And bandage the fractures of my heart
Amidst the silence of the trees
Give me the strength to heal

Life Will Find You Again

There are times
When something hits you in the guts
And you get the wind knocked out of you
Good and proper.
The sense of certainty
That all your hard work
Will pay off
Drops out of your hand
And shatters on the hard ground
Right next to your body.

Your achievements
And your goals
Suddenly feel tainted.
You lose faith
In your capabilities.
You feel foolish
You ever had dreams.

You seek solitude,
Because you are wounded and raw.
The image of you
Walking into the sea
And sinking to the bottom
Is strangely soothing.
But the world and its demands
Haul you back to the surface.

You switch from living to functioning.

When you hear something positive and uplifting
You feel too numb
To let it close,
Let alone touch you.

But a seed gets sown
And somewhere in the back of your brain
A little voice whispers:

It's only a phase.
Life will find you again.

Love Endures

Love endures loss
Love endures longing
Love endures limbo

Love endures hope
Love endures humiliation
Love endures hurt

Love endures disappointment
Love endures dejection
Love endures despair

Love endures yearning
Love endures promises
Love endures betrayal

Love endures silence
Love endures distance
Love endures indifference

Love endures falling out
Love endures falling back in
Love endures love

Love endures

Morning Walks

One
Toddling
Behind.

One
Strutting
Out front.

Me
In the middle
Pretending
To be
Top dog.

Most Days

He never touches me.
Not a hug or a caress down my back,
A peck on the cheek, a kiss in my hair.
Not an arm around my shoulders
Or a desire to hold my hand.

He shows his love
In cooking wholesome meals,
Coaching the kids' cricket team,
Holding a steady job.

His love
Anchors me in high winds,
Is firm underfoot when I explore,
Keeps the home fires burning whilst I am away.

He loves me
With humour
And patience
And insights outside the square.

Most days it's enough.

Mother Talk

I am a mother
You are a mother
It shows in our talk
Our eyes acknowledge each other
I think what if?
What if it happened to me
To my little ones, to my family
Could I hold out hope
Or would I crumble and cry
I would surely feel dead
Before I die

Thoughts about the Stolen Generations

My Silence

Forgive my silence.

My throat is empty like my heart.
I have no words to occupy my mind.
My tongue forms not a single phrase to pass the threshold of my lips.
I have no sound to let my vocal cords vibrate.
My oral cavity contains no conversation.

For every topic I hold dear
You counter with contempt.

No Such Thing

There's no such thing as a free lunch.
You see, from where I stand
We might have got the dog for free.
The fence cost us two grand.

Oh World, Retreat

Sand fills my every pore
Tiny shells tickle my toes
And minute particles of rock massage my soles.

A symphony of waves caresses my ears
The sweet tang of seaweed courts my nostrils
While boats on the horizon anchor my gaze.

My soul finds solace in the sandy mud
Where tide meets shore
My feet held tight in its embrace.

All the atoms that are me
Diffuse into a million molecules
Until I no longer exist.

I am earth, sand and water,
Wind and weed, birds and fish
As the wind lifts me to lightness.

Oh World, retreat!

Let me linger in this pocket of peace.
Let me savour the silence of the sea.
Even the birds honour the quiet of this hour.

Only Child

Give me air, let me breathe, give me space.
So what if I make a mistake.
Stop patronising and guiding me
wanting my best. Give it a rest.
Let me be quiet or loud, let me be proud
of who I am. Let me stand out.

Let me shine, let me fly, stop being embarrassed by
A daughter who chooses to challenge
Your little conventional world.
Let me be flamboyant and free.
Show some goddamn pride in me.
So what if I get into strife.
It's called life!

I know I am causing you trouble
In your little conservative bubble.
Your world is so perfect and fake,
Just give it a break, for God's sake.

Let me fly,

    Let me soar,

        Let me shine,

            Let me roar,

Let me be,

    Let me free,

        Be proud of me.

Puppy's First Walk

He pulls me here, he pulls me there,
He pulls me bloody everywhere.
He is out front and then behind,
Then by my side. We're quite a pair.

We finally make it to the park.
I feel him strain, I see him drool.
I use some treats to make him sit,
That's what we've learnt at puppy school.

As soon as he is off the lead
He spots some mates and he is gone.
Far at the oval's other end
He joins the gang and runs along.

He and his friends are having fun.
Some chase a ball, some chase a stick.
They piddle, sniff, and bark and run.
They roll and rumble, leap and lick.

He finally deigns to quit the game.
He comes and lays down by my feet.
My throat is sore from calling him.
He looks at me and then his treat.

We set off home at a slow pace,
He is too tired now to walk.
At some point he just stops and sits,
I end up carrying the dog.

He licks my face and wags his tail.
My heart near bursts with love and joy.
I whisper as I hold him tight,
'What a good boy. What a good boy.'

Regrets

Regrets I do have many, but life is life, it's what it is.
It cannot always be pure bliss.
You do your best with what you know,
Make your mistakes and let them go,
Live with the guilt the best you can,
A better human, woman, man.

Regrets I do have many, though lots of them are small.
Most of the time I can stand tall.
Alas, when lack of kindness on my part
Diminished you and scarred your heart,
That memory pains me most of all
And I will gladly take the fall.

Regrets I do have many, but please may God forbid
My time runs out, they close the lid,
Before I learn from what I did.
When I end up in deep dark earth,
I hope you feel my life was worth
My mother's pain when she gave birth.

Siberia

Everyone is connected
I am out in the cold
I can't reach anyone
No one can reach me

I am in a bubble
Impenetrable invisible
Even if I wanted to communicate
I would not be heard

It is not even my fault.
It's a faulty sim card.

So Be It

I don't care about black or white,
Yellow, red or brown.
What I am looking for in a fellow human being
Is decency, integrity, and generosity of spirit.

It doesn't matter if you are gay or queer,
Disabled, disfigured or disadvantaged.
That's not to say that my comfort zone will never go unchallenged.
I am honest about my limitations.

A wrong cannot be wrong for some
And less wrong for others.
Rape is rape, wherever you come from.
A lie is a lie, not matter what system you grew up in.

Feel free to worship as you see fit.
But please don't preach to me about religion.
My spiritual persuasion is personal.
It is mine and mine alone.

My skin gives me privileges and responsibilities.
I acknowledge the hurt my race has caused.
Sorry is a powerful word.
But I no longer wish to be held responsible for all the woes in the world.

I am interested in your story and who you are.
Maybe we'll like each other, maybe we won't.
But please don't paint me into a corner and attach labels.
I wish to be free to judge a book by its content, not its cover.

I have got a million questions and very few answers.
But please let me explore life from all angles,
Not just follow the flavour of the month.
I no longer wish to be gagged by political correctness.

The truth is, I no longer believe in a perfect world.
I no longer wish to fight wars for others.
Instead I want to keep peace in my own little orb.
If you disagree, so be it.

I wrote this poem after I had been part of a conversation about several issues of importance. I suddenly found myself in the opposing camp after voicing some doubts about various popular views. In the increasingly polarised discussion I kind of split in half, part of me was still engaged in the conversation, the other part became an observer of the ensuing dynamics. I realised how easy it is to become marginalised. At some point the fact that we are all human beings was strongly emphasised and I wondered where in the proceedings I had given the impression that I did not share this view. I believe that generalisation and sentimentality are unproductive. To me, an Us and Them attitude does not seem conducive to finding solutions. I have no specific religious or political affiliations and simply endeavour to live by my own high standards in the hope that the greater part of who I am keeps being motivated by kindness and compassion.

Strong

I am strong.

Not now.
Not at the moment.
Not today.
But I was in the past
And I will be again.

Tomorrow.

When a decision needs to be made.

The Bonds of Guilt

YOU

Unsettled me with your unpredictability Shackled me with your sadness Restrained me with your resentment Daunted me with your demands Suffocated me with your self-righteousness Tormented me with your tirades Mangled me with your manipulations Arrested me with your anger Persecuted me with your prejudice Jarred me with your judgements Imprisoned me with your imperiousness Incarcerated me with your inconsistencies Slashed me with your self-pity Hit me with your hate

BUT

Your nets of regret catch me no longer
Your sea of silence drowns me no more
Your ropes of reproach hold me no longer
Your ties of misery martyr no more

Your bonds of guilt have frayed

BECAUSE

I am not you.

You are not me.

This is my life.

I choose to be free.

The Bridges of Madison County

You're all I ever wanted
And it could never be
I could not shift a mountain
I could not drain the sea

You took me and you held me
When we turned out the lights
We slipped under the darkness
For a few stolen nights

One morning you got up
Because you had to leave
I closed the door and found a box
To store away my grief

Then my old life came walking
Right back through the same door
Tempted I was to throw it
Away across the floor

But I've held onto it and stayed
And lived as best I knew
Whilst every night before I sleep
I send a star to you

The Gift of Menopause

Blood flows dark and sluggish
From a waning womb
The realisation
That reproductive responsibilities
Can be put to rest
Dawns on you
As the world opens its window wide
To creativity of a another kind
The land of Self is beckoning
With a smile and the promise of pure delights
Winter becomes your season
And airflow a necessity
You dread days over 25
But nothing quenches the joy in children
Who like you are
Finding their own way.

The Gift of Silence

I give you the gift of Silence
Of words that don't have to be said
Of conversations that don't have to be had

I give you the gift of Silence
The gift of the absence of sound
Of noise that doesn't have to be drowned

I give you the gift of Silence
Of comments that don't have to be made
Of music that doesn't have to be played

I give you the gift of Silence
Of communication that need not be heard
Of understanding without a word

I give you the gift of Silence
Of sound that doesn't need to be killed
Of space that doesn't need to be filled

I give you the gift of

Their Land We Walk

Their land we walk
Ochre red dirt
Under white feet
Ploughing through country
We take we don't talk

> Without treaties or contracts
> We took what was theirs
> Without sorry or thought
> We pass it on to our heirs

Their land we use
Breaking Earth's skin
And digging deep
Wounds that won't heal
In the end we all lose

> With little attempt
> To make right what was wrong
> We debate we discuss
> Make them wait far too long

Their land we farm
Creating great wealth
But unwilling to share
What nature provides
In the depth of its palm

> Without remorse or regret
> We can't reconcile
> What our ancestors did
> In colonial style

On their land we've built
Cities and towns
Into blue sky
We close eyes and ears
As we fear our guilt

> If we don't honour Country
> And stay deaf to its Song
> If we don't respect Spirit
> We will never belong

It's their land we walk
Ochre red dirt
Under white feet
Let's acknowledge the hurt
Then sit down and talk

Threesome

In those days
when we
still had morning quickies

we
forgot to close
the door one time.

Once we
reached the point of
no return
puppy came bounding in

thinking
that all
this morning exercise
was great fun.

Three tongues
eight legs
and a waggy tail.

Happy days!

Too Old, Too Short

For John

I am too old
To be
Sensible reliable predictable

I am too old
To
Behave be nice fit in

I am too old
To be
Modest careful quiet

I am too old
To
Please bow kowtow

I am too old
To care about
Conformity consequences criticism

I am too old
To worry about
Regulations reputations expectations

I am too old
To follow
Rules courtesies conventions

I am too old
Not to be
Who I am.

Life is too short.

Turned to Stone

How much in our lives are lies
How much do we conceal
How many things get never talked about

How often do we wear a mask
To cover how we feel
And hope we may discover a way out

We separate our inner selves
From who we are outside
How quick are we to make that sacrifice

How often do we acquiesce
How often do we hide
Without admitting that we pay a price

How often do we pray at night
So desperate for advice
And when we wake up we are still alone

We bury our dreams inside
And never even realise
Somewhere along the way we turned to stone

Widow

Pencilled eyebrows
Perfect from years of practice
Hot pink lips
Matching the colour of the collar
On her navy top
Shoes, navy and grudgingly sensible,
Sinking into stray clumps of still fresh soil
Flowers in fingers with bands of gold
Only one has meaning now
Too late

Winter Sun

No soccer today.
Time for a little sleep-in until the dogs demand their morning walk.
        No bye here.
The sun greets us and I open my zip halfway.
        The house is still quiet when we come back.
The aromas of damp fur and hot coffee mingle as we all settle in front of the fire.
The washing should dry on the line today.
        The forecast said so.

www.ingramcontent.com/pod-product-compliance
Lightning Source LLC
Chambersburg PA
CBHW062204100526
44589CB00014B/1951